CHITA

High-Performance Operations

Leader Training

Make More Money - *Faster!*

Paul Brainard

Tree Free Press
La Verne, California

Published by:

Tree Free Press
La Verne, California 91750

ChitaHPO.com

First Edition 2013

Library of Congress Control Number: 2013948883

ISBN 978-0-9761193-5-7

Manufactured in the United States of America

Cover design and illustrations by Lily Brainard

Table of Contents

The Chita Program - *Introduction*

Make More Money! Faster!

The purpose of this course is to **train managers** to lead the **Chita-High Performance Operations** program in their organizations.

- The **Chita** program is a **simple** and **reliable** way to improve your organization's **profitability** while creating a culture of **continuous improvement**.

- **Chita** joins process **operators** with **management**, to construct a powerful operations improvement alliance.

- **Chita** precisely focuses **effort** and **resources** on activities that will **improve profits and cash flow**.

- Operators and managers **learn by doing**, and improvement to your operations will begin shortly after the program is started.

The goals of the Chita program:

1. Assist your organization in rapidly improving operations:

- Increase **throughput** and sales.
- Reduce costs.
- **Increase profits & cash flow**.
- Elevate your competitive position.

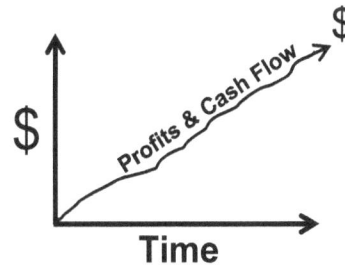

2. Empower & motivate your process operators:

- **More control** over their jobs.
- **Increased value** to company.
- Opportunity to **earn more**.
- Greater job **satisfaction**.

3. Create a culture of continuous process improvement:

- Operators view the tasks they perform as **processes**.
- Management and operators **join together** to continuously improve the processes, in **small steps**.
- Customers, management, operators and owners **all benefit** from improved operations.

Leading Operations

What is leadership?

- **Directing** people to perform activities that support the organization's mission.
- **Empowering** them with tools and skills, to perform the activites better and faster.
- **Motivating** them to perform the activities.

What is your company's mission?

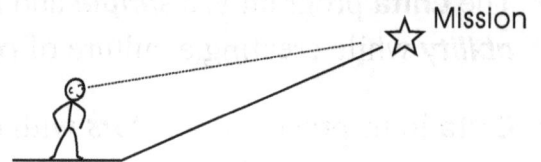

Mission

Directions from different organizational levels.

Each level of an organization serves different purposes and plays different roles in determining the direction of the organization:

- **Mission** - The purpose of the organization.
- **Strategic** - What products or services will be sold and what markets to sell to.
- **Tactical** - Where products or services will be created and the channels of distribution.
- **Operations** - Creating and distributing the products or services.

Chita focuses on the operations level.

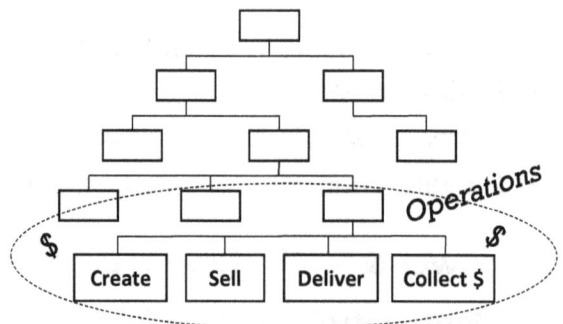

Operations

Create | Sell | Deliver | Collect $

Operations consists of _processes_ that:

- **Develop & Produce** products or services.
- **Sell** products or services.
- **Deliver** products or services.
- **Collect** payment for products or services.

The operations level is critical:

- Where all **goods** and **services** we enjoy are created.
- Where all profits, **wealth** and gross domestic product are created.
- **Problems** or disruptions are costly.
- Immense **opportunity** for increasing company profits.

Directing Operations

In what direction should an organization's operations move?

Continuous process improvement is an effective way to:

- Improve product or service *quality*.
- Increase product or service *throughput*.
- Increase *sales*.
- Reduce *costs*.
- Increase *profits* and *cash flow*.

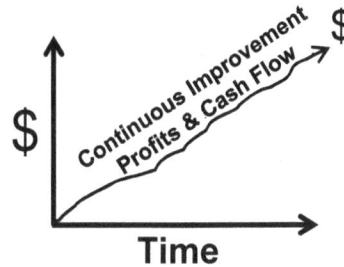

If fully implemented, *Continuous Process Improvement* is an effective direction for an organization's operations.

How important are profits and cash flow to your company?

Conventional direction for operations:

- Driven from the *top downward*.
- Often uses a *trial and error* approach.
- Frequently relies on *coercive* motivation.

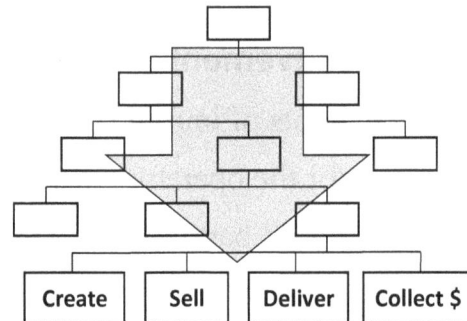

Chita works differently. Process *operators* actively *participate* in the improvement of operations.

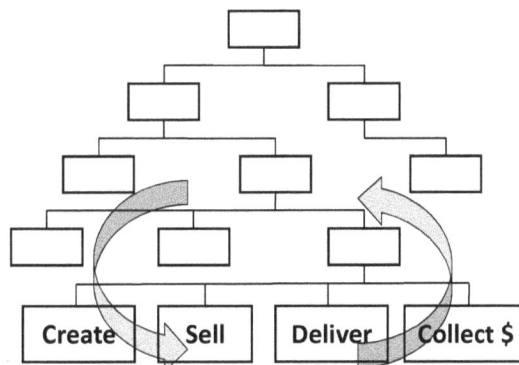

How much do your operators participate in decisions that affect operations?

Operator Participation

Process operators should participate in process improvement:

- Operators have the greatest hands-on **working knowledge** of the processes.
- They can provide much of the critical **information** needed for improving the processes.
- They offer different **perspectives**, to generate **more ideas** for improving the processes.
- Participation will **motivate** them to support and **press** for implementation of improvement.

How many operators do you have in your company? In which direction would you like them to push?

Process improvement is usually best done in small steps:

- The benefits of improvement can be enjoyed **faster**.
- Easier for the operators to **participate**.
- Easier for all participants to **visualize** each step.
- **Predictable** outcomes.
- **Less risk**.
- **Lower** up-front **cost** and investment.

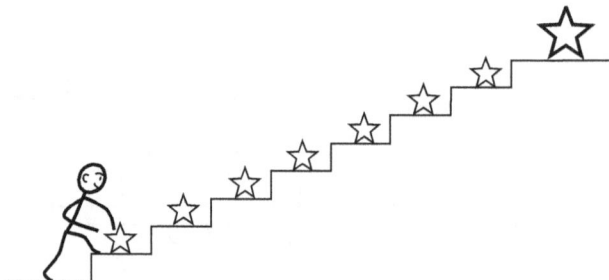

*Have you ever participated in, or witnessed a management **drive** to improve operations and profits? Were the outcomes of the **drive** better or worse than expected?*

Planning the Chita Operator Training

The **Chita** course and *operator workbook* were developed to *direct, empower and motivate* process operators to improve the processes they work with daily.

The <u>Operator Workbook</u> introduces operators to basic process improvement tools:

- Operators learn that the tasks they perform are *processes*.
- Explains how the operators will *benefit* from better processes.
- Gives them tools they can use to confidently improve processes.

<u>Leader Training</u> - *Study the operator workbook:*

- *Review* the workbook to ensure that you understand all the concepts that will be presented to the operators.

<u>Leader Action</u> - *Schedule the training:*

- Determine how to break up the operators into *groups* for the training.
  - The members of each group should *work together* in the same area of operations.
  - *Group size* should be taken into consideration. If the group is too large, it may be difficult for all members to participate.
- Plan to meet *once a week*, with each work cell or group, for one-half hour.
- To minimize disruption, I prefer to have *lunch meetings*. The company buys the operators lunch, they give up their time.
- Tell them that you want to hear *their ideas* for improving their work areas.

How will your operators respond to your invitation to attend a lunch meeting to solicit their ideas?

Planning the Chita Operator Training

Leader Action - *Supplies for class:*

- Large *whiteboard*.

- Large *paper pad* on *easel* to make lists or draw diagrams that you will want to keep for later reference.

- Several *dry erase markers* of different colors.

- One copy of the *Chita*-**Operator Workbook** for each participating operator.

- *Pedometers*.

- *Projector* to display the training slides.

How much would your company need to invest to start the Chita program?

Session 1 - *Process Problems*

In the first session you will initiate six simple activities:

1. ***Ask*** the operators to ***divulge*** any problems with the processes.
2. ***Listen*** to their responses.
3. Start a ***problem list.***
4. Define what a ***process*** is.
5. ***List*** some of the organization's processes.
6. ***Discuss*** the **Chita** program.

Class Activity 1 - *Identifying process problems:*

- After one or two operators have sat down, ask the operators something like: ***"What are some of the problems we have with the processes that you work with?"***

- Using the easel pad, start a list of process problems.

Listen! - This is your opportunity to ***engage*** and emotionally ***involve*** the operators in the program. Focus on ***encouraging*** the operators to mention any problems or concerns they see, not problems you see. You can add your own concerns to the list later on.

- ***Add*** to the problem list each week as you progress through the workbook.

- The problem list will be discussed again in Class Exercise 10.

- If the question ***"What is a process?"*** arises, jump to page 8 of the workbook, to begin defining what a process is.

- Discuss the purpose of the **Chita** program in terms of your ***organization's needs***, and honestly explain how meeting the organization's needs will ***benefit the operators***. Page 7 of the workbook.

Does your company need to: Improve quality?
Increase sales?
Reduce costs?
Increase profits or cash flow?

How should the operators benefit from their contribution to continuous improvement of profits and cash flow?

Session 1 - *Process Defined*

What is a Process?

- Read page 8 of the workbook.

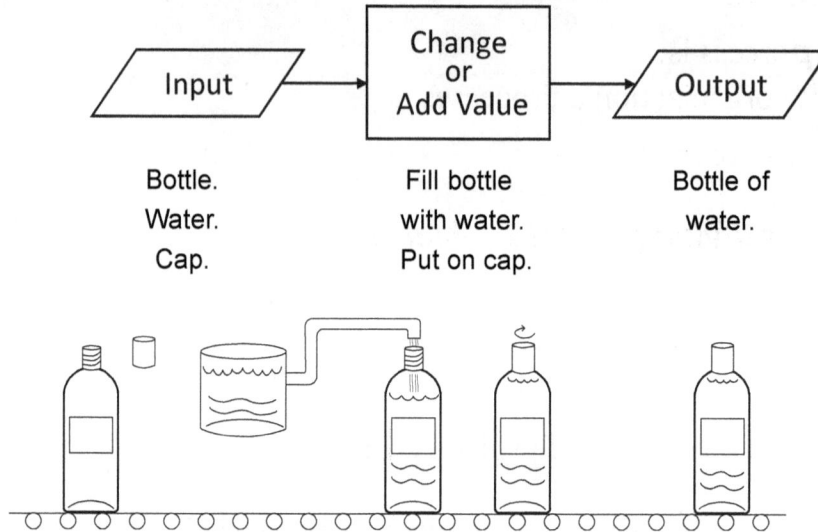

Input	Change or Add Value	Output
Bottle. Water. Cap.	Fill bottle with water. Put on cap.	Bottle of water.

Class Exercise 1 - *Identify existing processes.*

- The operators will *identify* some of the processes they work with.

- Select some of the processes listed, and write down the *inputs, changes and outputs* on the whiteboard.

Completing the class exercises.

- Class exercises can be done in class or out of class as homework.

- Some exercises, like Class Exercise 1, may be best done in class to reinforce the learning.

- Asking the operators to complete some exercises outside of class will speed up completion of the program.

Session 2 - *Flowcharts*

Using *flowcharts* to document a process.

- Read page 10 of the workbook.
  - *Flowchart symbols* and what they represent.
  - Why flowcharts are *useful*.

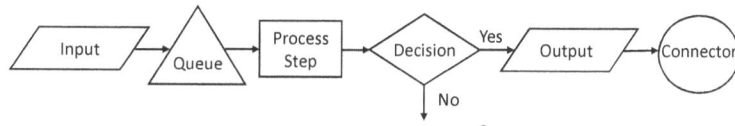

- Read page 11 of the workbook.
  - *Summary flowchart* of a paint chair process.

  - *Detailed flowchart* of the same paint chair process.

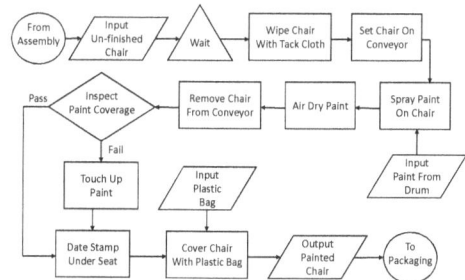

Class Exercises 2 & 3 - *Documenting a process.*

- *Select* one of the processes listed in *Class Exercise 1*.
- On the whiteboard or paper pad, *draw a summary flowchart* of the process.
- Next, *draw a detailed flowchart* of the process.

Session 3 - *Work Flow Diagram*

Class Exercise - *Draw a work flow diagram of the work cell:*

- On the whiteboard, draw a rough diagram of the entire **work cell layout**.
- Draw **triangles** to show where **materials are waiting**. This will be important information when you start working on improving cycle time and throughput.
- **Draw** a different colored line for each possible work flow.

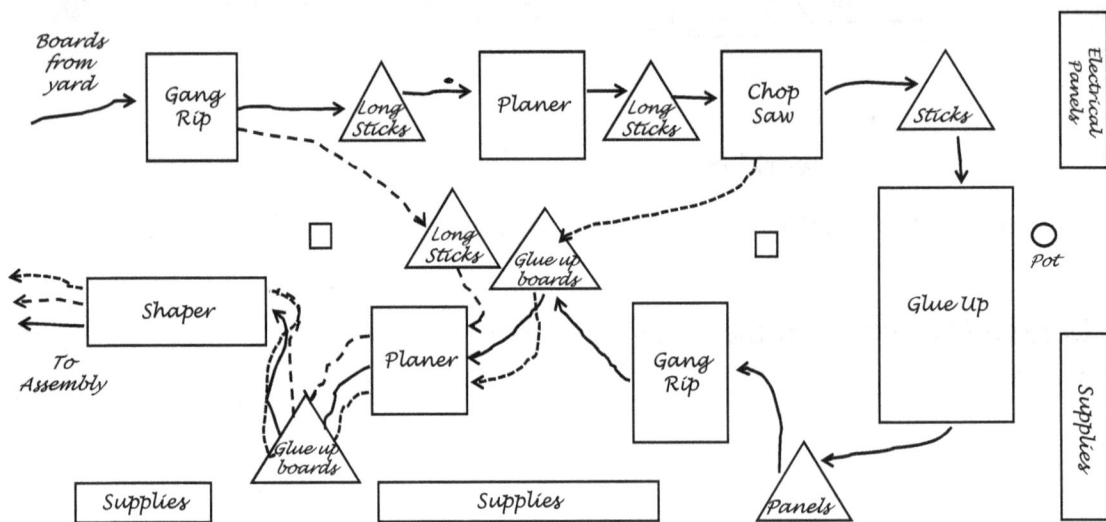

Look for low-hanging fruit:

- Do the layout and work flows make sense?
- Can the layout or work flows be improved to **reduce** operator **motion** or material movement?
- Look for low hanging fruit. **Easy** to make **changes** that will make the work easier.
- Do **not** invest much time or money to rearrange a work area at this stage of the program. If a major rearrangement is needed, it will be much easier to do it later in the course.

Opportunities for improving processes:

- The work flow diagram will help you to spot opportunities to **reduce** operator **motion**.
- The triangles show where **materials** are sitting and **waiting**; opportunities for reducing cycle time and inventory, while increasing throughput. Discussed later.

Session 4 - *Measuring Process Performance*

Seven process performance metrics

To determine if a process is *improving*, process *performance metrics* are needed. *Chita* uses *seven metrics* to determine if a process is improving. The operators will learn how to use some simple tools for improving processes in terms of the metrics.

↓ **Injuries** - The number of employee injuries during a period of time.

↑ **On-Time Performance** - The percentage of process outputs that are completed correctly and on schedule.

↓ **Cycle Time** - The time it takes for inputs to become outputs.

↑ **Throughput** - The amount of output a process can create during a period of time.

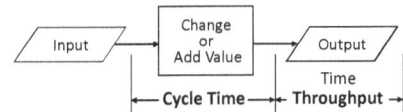

↓ **Variability** - The consistency of process inputs, process activities and outputs.

↓ **Inventory** - The amount of inventory within a process.

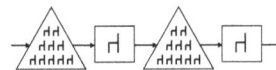

↓ **Cost** - The money spent on process inputs and process activities.

These basic metrics will provide clear and objective *direction* for improving the processes.

Class Exercise 4 - *Identify existing process metrics.*
- On the whiteboard, list any *existing* process *metrics*.
- For each metric listed, determine if it measures any of the *seven dimensions* described above.
- Who currently calculates and reports the metric?
- Who sees the reporting of the metric?

Session 5 - *Injuries & Run Charts*

Introduction to run charts

We will use the *injury metric* to introduce the operators to *run charts*, *Pareto charts* and *root cause* analysis.

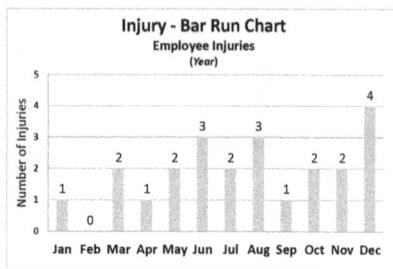

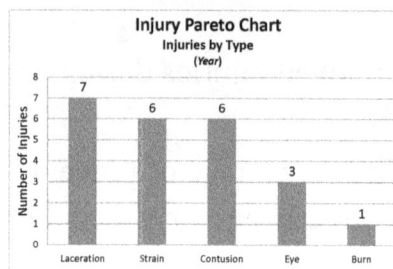

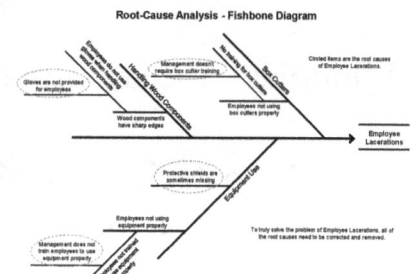

Run charts are a simple way to *visually communicate* the history and trend of each of the seven metrics. Run charts are used to track and communicate the *progress* made when improving processes.

The charts can easily be produced and updated using a spreadsheet program.

Leader Preparation - *Injury data*

- **Collect** the injury data needed for exercises 5 through 8 of the course workbook.
  - A list of all the injuries for the prior twelve months, that includes the date and a description of each injury.
- **Invite** the person who keeps track of the injury data to attend the class to present the data to the operators.

Class Exercise 5 - *Injury history.*

- Present injury history data to operators.
- A list of the injuries showing the date and description of each injury.

Class Exercises 6 & 7 - *Measuring injuries using run charts.*

- Using the injury data, *draw a bar run chart*.
- Using the same injury data, *draw a line run chart*.

Problem Elimination Tools

Two major ways to improve processes:

- **Problem elimination** - Identifying and removing problems such as injuries.
- **Innovation** - New ideas for improving processes in terms of the seven metrics.

Start with problem elimination:

- It's *easy* for operators to *identify* problems.
- Eliminating the problems that frustrate the operators, will get the operators *emotionally involved* in the program.
- It will be a source of *motivation* for the operators to improve the processes.

Some ways to identify problems:

- **Listen** to operator concerns and complaints.
- Pareto chart of *on-time performance failures*. Discussed more in 'On-Time Performance'.
- Pareto chart of *customer complaints* and returns. Discussed more in 'Variability'.
- Pareto chart of process *rejects*. Discussed more in 'Variability'.
- Pareto chart of process *down time*. Discussed more in 'Cycle Time'.
- Pareto chart of operator *injuries*. Discussed more in 'Class Exercise 8'.

Session 6 - *Problem Elimination-Pareto Charts*

Ranking and prioritizing problems

- Managers often become *overwhelmed* in responding to the many problems that arise, making it difficult to resolve each problem so that the problem doesn't reoccur.

- They often slap a *bandage* on the problem and *move on* to the next problem.

- Ranking and *prioritizing* problems using a Pareto chart helps management to stay focused on the critical problems long enough to *permanently correct* the problems.

- Problems should also be prioritized based on *operator input*.

- Operator *participation* in problem solving will *speed up* the process of problem elimination.

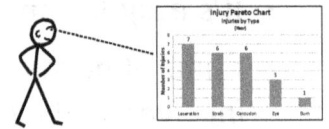

Are there any reoccurring problems in your operations?

Class Exercise 8 - *Ranking injury types using a Pareto chart.*

- Using the injury data from *Class Exercise 5*, the operators will make a *list of the types* of injuries and show the quantity of each type.

- After making the list, they will draw a *Pareto chart* of the injuries.

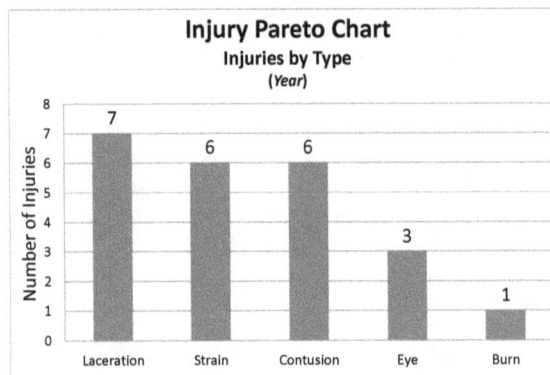

Injury Pareto Chart
Injuries by Type
(Year)

Injury Type	Number of Injuries
Laceration	7
Strain	6
Contusion	6
Eye	3
Burn	1

Session 7 - *Problem Elimination-Root Cause*

Eliminating problems

To truly correct a problem, the **root causes** need to be identified and removed. A **fishbone diagram** facilitates the root cause analysis process.

Fishbone Diagram

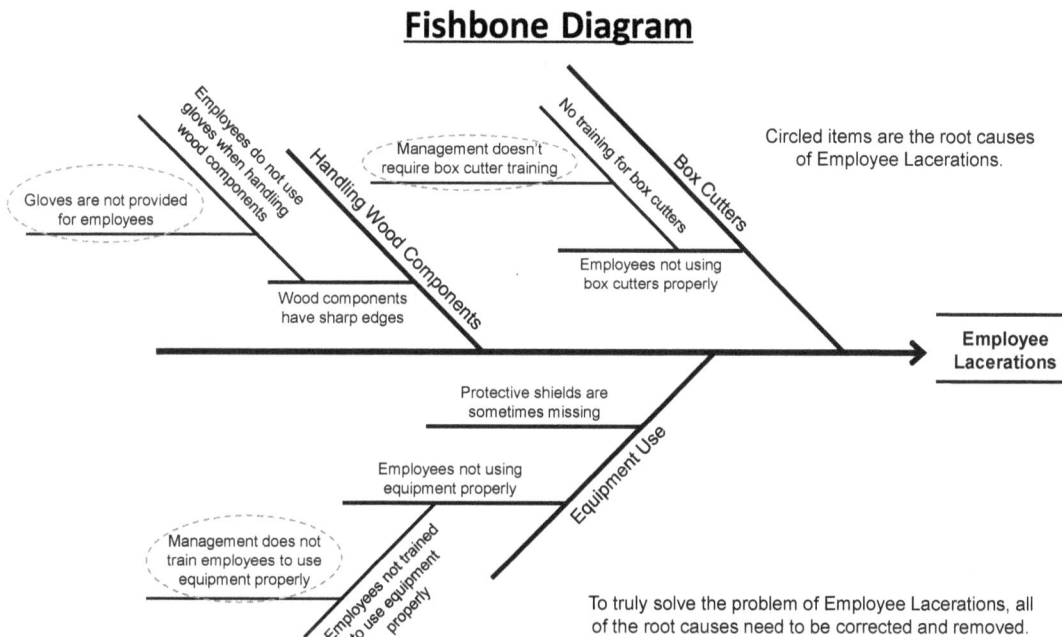

Employees do not use gloves when handling wood components

Gloves are not provided for employees

Handling Wood Components

Management doesn't require box cutter training

No training for box cutters

Box Cutters

Circled items are the root causes of Employee Lacerations.

Wood components have sharp edges

Employees not using box cutters properly

Employee Lacerations

Protective shields are sometimes missing

Employees not using equipment properly

Equipment Use

Management does not train employees to use equipment properly

Employees not trained to use equipment properly

To truly solve the problem of Employee Lacerations, all of the root causes need to be corrected and removed.

Fishbone diagrams are useful for:

- *Identifying* all the root-causes of a complex problem that has multiple root-causes.
- *Communicating* to others the root-causes of a problem.
- *Brainstorming* on a problem as a group.
- *Determining* the corrective actions needed to remove the problem.

Class Exercise 9 - *Analyzing and correcting injuries.*

- Select the **most common** type of injury from the Pareto chart drawn in **Class Exercise 8**.
- Draw a **fishbone diagram** to identify the **root causes** of the most common type of injury.
- Develop **corrective action plans** (what, who & when) to remove each root cause.
- If it's hard to agree on an action plan, maybe the root cause has not been identified, and you should continue to drill down by asking "Why?".

Problem Elimination

Leader Preparation - *More problem elimination.*

- ***Each week*** add to the list of problems and concerns. ***Cross off*** any problems that have been corrected.

- A good way to ***start every meeting*** is to ask the operators if they see any new problems that should be added to the problem list.

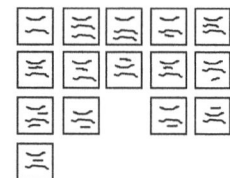

- Each problem is an ***opportunity for improvement***, so list as many as possible.

- Invite someone from sales to attend a meeting and add to the list any ***customer complaints***.

- For each problem listed, indicate the ***impact*** (seriousness) of the problem as small, medium or large, and the estimated ease or ***cost to fix*** the problem as low, medium, or high.

- Look for any ***relationships*** among the problems, to find common root causes. One way to do this is to write each problem on a ***slip of paper***, and organize by root cause.

Push on:

- ***Don't get discouraged*** as the list of problems grows larger and larger. Each problem is a golden ***opportunity*** for improvement. The larger the list, the greater the opportunity to improve the processes.

- Do ***not*** try to resolve the problems as they are listed. Just ***add to the list and move on***. Focus on completing the workbook. Many of the problems will be eliminated as you progress through the workbook.

- When you choose to tackle one of the problems, ***set aside a meeting*** to do a ***root cause analysis*** and commit to ***action plans*** that will correct the root causes.

Motivating operators:

- It is critical that ***some*** of the problems get fixed ***promptly*** so that the operators can see that this program will improve their work, otherwise they may see it as more empty management talk.

- ***Start with problems that can be easily fixed.***

Session 8 - *Problem Elimination Exercise*

Assigning action items.

- *What* needs to be done, as determined by the completed fishbone diagram?
- *Who #1* has the greatest *knowledge* needed to complete the action item?
- *What resources* will be needed, including employee time?
- *Who #2* in *management* will ensure the resources are made available?
- *When* will each action item be complete?

The two people assigned should be jointly accountable for completing the action item.

Assigning the person with the best knowledge and ensuring that the necessary resources are made available, creates a high probability that the action item will be completed successfully.

Follow up & recognition.

- When the action items are *complete*, did the problem go away?
- If *not*, review the fishbone diagram for *missed* root causes.
- If the problem *did* go away, give *recognition* to everybody who participated.

Class Exercise 10 - *Analyzing and correcting problems.*

- Select one problem that has a *large impact* and will have a *low cost* to fix.
- Have the operators identify the *root causes* of the problem using a fishbone diagram.
- Develop corrective *action plans* (what, who & when) to remove each root cause.
- Identify what process *performance metrics* will be improved.
- *Implement* each action plan.
- *Follow up* to determine if the action plans worked as expected.

Session 9 - On-Time Performance

On-time performance

On-time performance measures the percentage of customer orders that are completed *correctly* and *on schedule*. On-time performance is one measure of variability. It is measured separately because of its importance to customers, external and internal.

If your customers receive their orders *on-time* and *correctly*:

- They will be *pleased*.
- They will continue to *buy* from the company.
- They will *refer* you to other potential customers.

If your customers receive their orders *late* or the orders are *not correct*:

- They will be *upset*.
- You risk *losing* them.
- You risk getting a *bad reputation*.

To *calculate* on-time performance, divide the quantity of orders that are completed correctly and on schedule by the quantity of all orders scheduled:

On-Time Performance = Qty of Correct & On-Time Orders / Qty of All Orders

The problem elimination tools discussed earlier are used to increase on-time performance:

- Run charts
- Pareto charts
- Root cause analysis fishbone diagrams

Increasing on-time performance:

- Begin *measuring* on-time performance and create a run chart.
- Identify and *track* on-time performance *failures*:
  - Customer orders that ship *later* than scheduled.
  - Orders that are *incorrect* for any reason.
  - For each failure, list the *reason why* the order was late or incorrect.
- Prepare a *Pareto chart* of on-time failure events.
- Do *root cause* analyses of each on-time failure starting with the highest ranking failure type.

Session 9 - *On-Time Performance*

Class Exercise 11 - *On-time performance run chart.*

Invite an employee who would have the data to calculate on-time performance. (The month to date quantity of orders scheduled to be delivered to customers, and the quantity of orders that were delivered on schedule and correctly.) Ask the employee to present the data to the operators, so the operators can calculate on-time performance.

The run chart in the exercise needs only to be done by the employee who is closest to the on-time performance data. Typically a customer service employee.

Class Exercise 12 - *On-time performance Pareto chart.*

Have the invited employee mentioned in exercise 11, complete Class Exercise 12 and create a Pareto chart for on-time performance failures. Ask the employee to present the Pareto chart to the operators.

Session 10 - *On-Time Performance-Root Cause*

Class Exercise 13 - *On-time performance root cause analysis.*

Select an on-time performance failure reason from Class Exercise 12, that the work cell affects, and have the operators draw a root cause fishbone diagram for that failure reason.

Assign action items for each root cause.

Session 11 - *Cycle Time*

Cycle time

Cycle time is the time it takes for inputs of a process to become outputs.

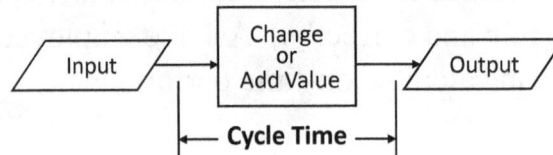

Reducing cycle time is ***not*** about pushing the process operators to work harder and faster, it's about improving the processes to make them more ***streamlined*** and more ***reliable***.

Reducing cycle time can:

- Increase ***throughput*** and sales.
- Reduce in-process ***inventory,*** increasing cash flow.
- Increase ***on-time performance***.
- Reduce labor ***costs***.
- Increase ***profits***, cash flow and return on investment.

Reducing cycle time is often the easiest and quickest way to improve an operation's ***profits and cash flow***.

Cycle time can be broken down into ***four components:***

- **Processing time** - The time spent modifying or ***adding value*** to inputs.

- **Queue time** - The time in-process ***materials*** sit idle ***waiting*** to be processed.

- **Setup time** - The time a process is idle while being readied for processing.

- **Down time** - The time a process is idle due to ***problems*** such as equipment failure.

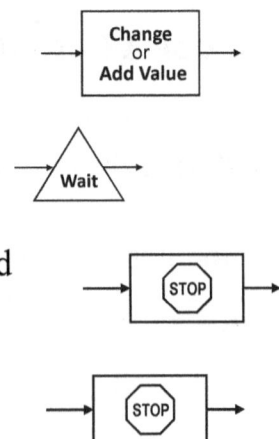

Cycle Time - *Process Formula*

The process formula, aka Little's Law, can be used to *calculate* cycle time:

Cycle Time = In-Process Inventory / Throughput

In-process inventory is the quantity of inventory that is *within the process.* *Throughput* is the amount of *output* a process creates during a period of time.

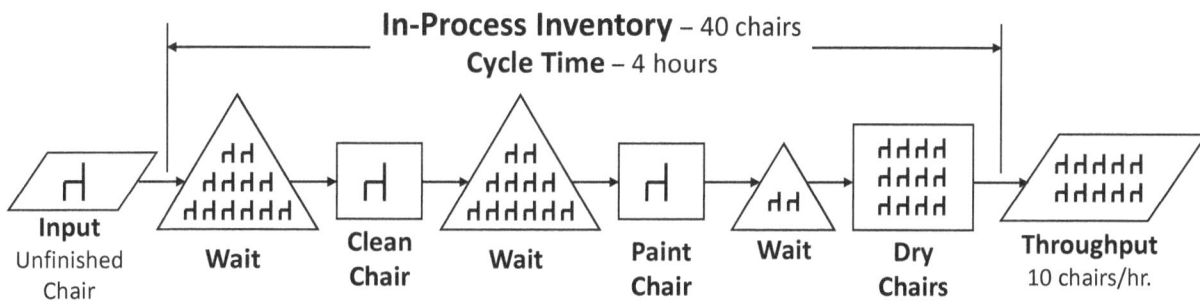

For example consider a chair painting process: If *in-process inventory is 40 chairs* at various stages of completion, and *throughput is 10 chairs per hour*, cycle time would be *4 hours*.

40 chairs / 10 chairs per hour = 4 hours

Anyone who works with processes, should *know this formula* well.

- The formula is useful for *spotting opportunities* to reduce cycle time. For example: the process formula shows that reducing in-process inventory by reducing batch size will reduce cycle time.

- The formula shows that whenever cycle time is improved, *throughput* or *inventory* will be *improved* as well.

- The formula is also useful for finding ways to *increase throughput* as we will see later when we discuss throughput.

Cycle Time

Class Exercise 14 - *Calculating cycle time.*

- Ask each operator to count the units of inventory in production within the process they flowcharted for *Class Exercises 2 & 3*.

    - Select the *first material component* input into the process and then count the quantity of the component present throughout the process.

    - Count **_all_** of the inventory that has been input into the process.

    - Note how much inventory is within *process steps* being modified, and how much of the inventory is sitting *waiting* for the next process step. This information will be used later for Class Exercise 27.

- What is the daily or hourly throughput for the same process?

- Divide the units in production by the throughput to get the cycle time.

- The calculation can be done using any time measurement: seconds, minutes, hours, days, months, etc. Which one is best, depends on the situation.

Class Exercise 15 - *Calculating cycle time for entire workcell.*

- Count all the units of production within a workcell.

- Divide by the daily or hourly throughput for the workcell.

- Start a run chart for cycle time and update monthly.

Can you combine Class Exercises 14 & 15?

Session 12 - Cycle Time-Value-Adding

Value-adding processes

Value-adding is creating **product features** or **services** that your customers **want** and are willing to **pay** for.

Examples of value-adding processes:

- **Filling** a clean bottle with clean water and **sealing** it with a secure cap.
- **Delivering** the bottles of water that your customer ordered to the right location, on time.

To determine what process steps add value, or to discover new ways to add value, **listen** carefully to your **customers**:

- What **features** are **important** to them? What features are **not important** to them?
- What **problems** do they have that you can help them solve?
- **Visit your customer's facility** to learn **how they use** your products or services.
- Invite your customers to **visit your facility** to meet with the operators, to discuss the **customer's needs** and expectations.

Non-value-adding activities are those activities that **do not directly** create product features or services that your customers want.

Examples of non-value-adding activities:

- Filling a **defective** bottle with **unclean** water and **loosely** putting on a cap.
- **Moving** boxes of bottles from the receiving dock to the bottle filling machine.
- **Setting up** the machine to begin filling bottles with water.
- **Searching** for a tool needed to set up the machine.
- Filling each bottle to the **brim** with water.
- **Repairing** the machine that fills the bottles with water.
- Operators **standing by** as the machine is fixed.
- **Stopping** the machine until a supervisor makes a **decision**.

Most activities in a company are **non-value-adding**, so there is a lot of opportunity to **reduce** the non-value-adding activities, in order to **reduce costs** and free up resources that can be used for value-adding processes.

Cycle Time - *Value-Adding*

Class Exercise 16 - *Value-adding & non-value adding activities.*

- To ensure the operators understand the difference between value-adding processes and non-value-adding activities, ask each operator to identify some of the ways that the process flowcharted in Class Exercise 3 *adds value* for your customers.

- Why are the customers willing to *pay* for the product features or services?

- Ask each operator to identify some of the *non-value-adding* activities of their work.

- Why are those non-value-adding activities *necessary?*

Cycle Time - *Non-Value-Adding*

Class Exercise 17 - *Non-value-adding movement.*

- Ask each operator to wear a pedometer for one day.

- Buy enough pedometers so that all the operators in a workcell can take a turn in a week's time.

- Ask each operator to report to you at the end of the day how many miles they walked, and give you the pedometer.

- Make a list showing the operator's name, date & miles walked.

Pedometer Log		
Date	Name	Miles Walked
4/18/13	Bill Jones	3.2
4/18/13	Jose Lopez	2.7
4/19/13	Steve Martin	7.3

- Total up the miles and report the total to them at the next meeting.

- Ask the operators how much of their walking was value-adding movement.

- Walking usually does not add value.

- Discuss why the walking was needed.

- Ask for suggestions to reduce the amount of walking, and create a list of the suggestions.

Session 13 - *Reducing Cycle Time*

Reducing Processing Time

Cleanliness & immaculate *organization* allows operators to be more nimble. This is also know as *5S*.

Simply *cleaning* and *organizing* work stations will:

- Reduce cycle time.
- Increase throughput.
- Reduce injuries.
- Reduce variability.
- Reduce costs.
- Increase on-time performance.
- Make the other process improvement activities much easier.

After problem-solving, *cleaning* and *organizing* work cells should be the next step in continuous process improvement:

- Anything *not necessary* to perform the process should be *moved out* of the work area.

- There should be an *assigned place* for everything needed.

- Needed *tools* should always be *easy to find* and *within reach*, by using tool storage like *shadowboards*.

- Anything that can be moved should have a *shadow*, to make it *visually obvious* when it is missing.

- Work areas should be *cleaned* often.

- Keep *personal belongings* in a *clean and secure* place out of the work area.

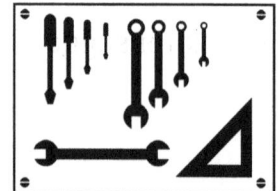

Encourage *creativity* in designing storage space. It can be *fun* designing tool storage using readily available, low cost materials.

- Start with at least *one* work area in each work cell.

- Find at least one operator that will *volunteer* to clean and organize his or her work station first.

- This will show the other operators the *benefits* of having a clean and organized work station, and other operators will likely want to do their work areas next.

Management needs to ensure that *resources*, including operator time, are made available to complete the cleaning and organizing.

Reducing Cycle Time

Non-value-adding activities

- First, identify all the value-adding tasks, then seek ways to eliminate or minimize all of the other non-value-adding activities.

- Design and organize work stations to minimize operator **motion**.

- Only some operator motion adds value. Identify the motions that add value, and seek ways to eliminate or minimize the non-value-adding motion.

- Using a **work flow diagram** of the work area, **brainstorm** with the operators to find ways to minimize the movement of inventory.

- **Conveyors** can be used to move inventory.

- **Rearrange** work cells to reduce operator motion.

- **Stage** materials next to operators to reduce operator walking.

Value-adding processes

- **Decision making** process steps can be shortened by **empowering operators** to quickly make commonly required decisions.

- **Combine process steps** so they can be performed **simultaneously** instead of sequentially.

- Use flowcharts to locate opportunities to perform process steps simultaneously.

- Make sure the **right tools** are being used for each task. Consult with suppliers to ensure that the proper tools are in use.

- **Automation technology** may be available to reduce processing time.

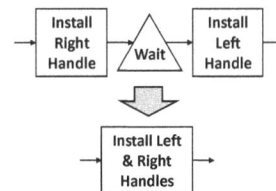

Session 14 - *Reducing Cycle Time*

Reducing Queue Time

Reducing queue time is often the **easiest** way to reduce cycle time **and** reduce inventory.

- Reduce the **transfer batch size** between process steps by using equipment such as conveyors.

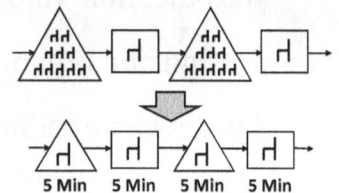

- **Balance** a process so that all process steps have the **same cycle time**.

- Identify and eliminate **bottlenecks** within the process. **Sessions 16 - 18** will discuss ways to remove bottlenecks.

- **Do not issue materials** to a production workorder, unless **all the materials** needed to complete the workorder are available.

Reducing Setup Time

Reducing setup time will increase **throughput**, leading to **more sales**.

Reducing setup time also allows **batch size** to be reduced, reducing cycle time and in-process inventory.

- Setup time can often be reduced by creating **specialized tooling** or jigs to speed up setup processes.

- Reduce the **processing time** of setup processes, by using the same methods discussed in **Session 13**.

- Compare the time it takes the **average driver** to change a tire to the time it takes in the pits of a **racetrack**.

Reducing Cycle Time

Reducing Down Time

Reducing down time will increase **throughput**, and **on-time performance**.

- When equipment goes down, **bells, lights** or **phones** can be used by operators to quickly communicate to maintenance personnel.

- **Maintenance** personnel should respond rapidly to down equipment.

- Down time can be reduced by improving **preventive maintenance** processes.

- Prepare a **Pareto chart** of the types of down time.

- Do a **root-cause analysis** for each type of down time as shown on the Pareto chart.

- Do the operators ever **stop** the processes to make decisions?

- **Empower operators** to quickly make frequently required decisions.

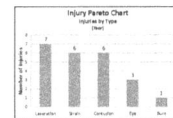

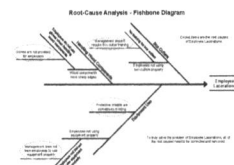

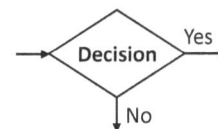

Class Exercise 18 - *Reducing cycle time.*

The operators have now been introduced to **several different tactics** for reducing cycle time:

- The operators will **identify** cycle time reduction tactics that could be used in their work areas.

- Each operator brings a different **perspective**, so each one may see different opportunities to use one or more of the cycle time reduction tactics discussed.

- Challenge each operator to think of **at least one** way to reduce the cycle time of the processes they work with.

Session 15 - *Throughput*

Throughput

Throughput is the amount of **outputs** a process can generate during a period of **time.**

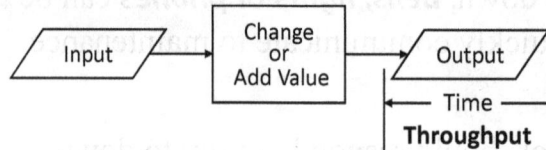

For example: - 10 chairs per minute.
- 100 chairs per hour.
- 10,000 bottles of water per day.

Just like reducing cycle time, *increasing throughput* is **not** about pushing the process operators to work harder and faster, it's about making the processes more **streamlined** and more **reliable**.

Increasing throughput:

- Allows *Sales* to increase.
- Reduces *Overtime* and costs.
- Increases *On-Time Performance*.
- Increases *Profits*.

The *first thing* we need to determine concerning process throughput:

➤ *Can process throughput keep up with the customer sales demand for the outputs, without overtime?*

- If the answer is: **Yes**, then there is *no need to increase* process throughput.

  - *Focus resources on increasing sales* by reducing costs, reducing variability and increasing on-time performance.

- If the answer is: **No**, then there is a *need to increase* process throughput.

Throughput - *Need to Increase?*

Class Exercise 19 - *Do we need to increase process throughput?*

The operators will **compare** the throughput of the process from earlier exercises to sales demand, to determine if throughput for the process needs to be increased.

- The operators will already know what the throughput is from **Class Exercise 14**.

- Invite someone from **sales** to present the sales demand data for the process outputs.

- There may be a need to **convert** the quantity of sales demand for finished product to the sales demand for the process outputs that are at an intermediate stage.

If throughput is equal to, or greater than, sales demand:

- Discuss how to increase sales demand by: - *Reducing costs,*
                                                          - *Reducing variability,*
                                                          - *Increasing on-time performance.*

- A representative from **sales** should **participate**.

- How to reduce **variability** and **costs** will be discussed later.

If throughput is less than sales demand:

Discuss how the company is **impacted**. Someone from sales should participate:

- Are there **lost sales?**

- Are customers upset about **late orders?**

- Is there a need for a lot of **overtime?**

How will the company and the operators **benefit** from increasing throughput?

- There will be higher **sales,**

- Greater **profits,**

- And more **profit sharing.**

Session 16 - *Bottleneck Management*

Bottleneck/Constraint management

A *bottleneck* process step, is the process step with the *lowest throughput* when compared to the other process steps within the process.

Bottleneck process steps *determine the throughput* of processes, so knowing how to *locate* and *remove* bottlenecks is key to increasing throughput.

- At any time, *one* bottleneck process step is restricting the throughput of the operation.

- Removing bottlenecks is usually the *quickest* and *lowest cost* way to increase capacity and throughput.

Locating bottleneck process steps:

- To locate bottleneck process steps, look for *accumulations* of in-process inventory. Inventory may pile up and wait in front of a bottleneck process step.

- Process steps *downstream* of a bottleneck process step may have to sit idle at times while waiting for the outputs of the bottleneck process step.

- Bottleneck process steps may require *overtime* hours of operation to keep up with the other processes.

- If the bottleneck is a *document process*, there will be a stack of paperwork before the bottleneck process step.

- For example: An office worker may not always generate the production work orders in a timely manner, making production wait and causing customer orders to be late.

Throughput - *Locating Bottlenecks*

In the example below, the **Paint Chair** process step is the bottleneck. Inventory is backed up waiting in front of the bottleneck process step. The downstream **Dry Chairs** process step is sometimes idle waiting for chairs.

The **throughput** of the **Paint Chair** process step is **10 chairs/hour**, and determines the throughput of the entire process.

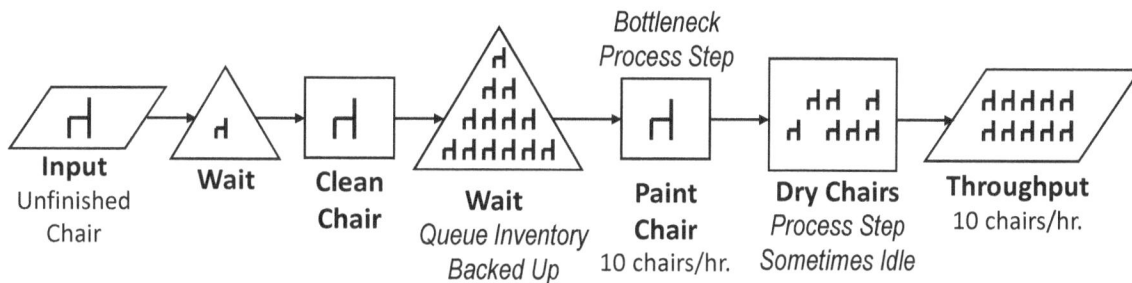

Class Exercise 20 - *Locating bottlenecks.*

The operators will review the detailed process **flowchart** from **Class Exercise 3,** and **locate** the process step that is the bottleneck. It will be the process step with the **lowest** throughput.

- Does inventory **accumulate** just **before** the bottleneck?

- Do any process steps regularly **sit idle** waiting to receive inventory from the previous process step?

- Do any process steps need to work **overtime** to keep up with the other process steps?

Throughput - *Process Formula*

The process formula rearranged

Rearranging the process formula that we discussed in **Session 11**, can help us to find ways to increase throughput:

Throughput = In-Process Inventory / Cycle Time

10 chairs per hour = 40 chairs / 4 hours

The formula shows us that:

- Reducing the ***processing time*** of a ***bottleneck*** process step will increase throughput.

- Reducing process ***down time*** will increase throughput.

- Reducing ***setup time*** will increase throughput.

- Increasing ***inventory*** without increasing cycle time will increase throughput.

We can use the ***same*** methods discussed in **Sessions 13 & 14** to reduce cycle time, setup time and down time, in order ***to increase throughput*** of the bottleneck process step.

Throughput - *Process Formula*

Class Exercise 21 - *Throughput & cycle time.*

The operators will use the process formula to see how reducing cycle time can increase throughput.

- Reducing cycle time by one-half and keeping in-process inventory the same will cause throughput to double.

20 chairs per hour = 40 chairs / 2 hours

- If you reduce cycle time by reducing *queue time* by one-half, in-process inventory will also be reduced by one-half, and throughput will remain the same.

10 chairs per hour = 20 chairs / 2 hours

To restate:

- Reducing *processing time, setup time* or *down time* will cause throughput to *increase*.
- Reducing *queue time* alone, will *reduce inventory* and throughput will remain the same.

We will discuss this further when we talk about how to reduce *in-process inventory*.

Session 17 - *Task Sheet*

To increase the throughput of a bottleneck process step:

1. **Prepare a *Task Sheet* listing all the tasks performed for the process step, that shows:**

   - Task sequence number.
   - Task description.
   - Cycle time of task.
   - The value-adding tasks.

Task Sheet: Paint Chair Process Step

Task #	Task Description	Cycle Time	How to Minimize	New Cycle Time
1	Set dolly on turntable	5 Seconds	Conveyor	0
2	Set chair on dolly	5 Seconds	Conveyor	0
3	Switch on turntable	2 Seconds	Footswitch	1 Second
4	Pick up spray gun from table	3 Seconds	No longer needed	0
5	Wipe nozzle with cloth	4 Seconds		4 Seconds
6	**Spray paint on chair back (VA)**	**9 Seconds**		**9 Seconds**
7	**Spray paint on seat (VA)**	**7 Seconds**		**7 Seconds**
8	**Spray paint on legs (VA)**	**8 Seconds**		**8 Seconds**
9	Set paint gun on table	3 Seconds	No longer needed	0
10	Switch off turntable	2 Seconds	Foot switch	1 Second
11	Roll chair to paint dry staging area	8 Seconds	Conveyor	0
	Total Cycle Time	**56 Seconds**		**30 Seconds**
	Value-Add	24 Seconds		24 Seconds
	Non-Value-Add	32 Seconds		6 Seconds

The process **operators** should prepare the **Task Sheet**, since they likely have the greatest working **knowledge** of the process.

- To determine the current task **cycle times**, operators may be able to **estimate** based on their experience, or **time studies** of the tasks can be performed.

- **Precise cycle times are not needed.** Estimates of the current and new cycle times should be adequate, and **effort should be focused on improving** the tasks. The **capacity sheet** discussed on **page 48** can be used to validate the estimates.

Throughput - *Task Sheet*

Time Studies

To do a **time study**, have someone **observe** the tasks as they are performed, and using a stopwatch, **measure** the time it takes for each task.

- The **operators should decide** whether a time study should be done. They should also choose the observer/timekeeper if they decide to do a time study.

- **Uninvited** time studies that are performed by managers or outsiders will **harm** operator **motivation**.

2. **Using the cycle time reduction methods discussed in Sessions 13 & 14, suggest ways to reduce the cycle time of each task. Estimate the new cycle time.**

- Set a **target** for the new cycle time. If throughput needs to increase by ten percent, the cycle time would need to be reduced by ten percent.

- Precise estimates of the new cycle times are not necessary. Effort should be focused on **implementing** the improvements.

- The actual amount of increased throughput will **validate** the estimates.

- Operator estimates should **improve** as they gain experience using the task sheets.

Initially focus on reducing non-value-adding tasks:

- Typically most tasks are non-value-adding, so there is usually more **opportunity** for reducing the cycle time of non-value-adding tasks.

- For value-adding tasks, the initial focus should be on improving quality by **reducing variability**. Discussed later.

- When reducing the cycle time of value-adding tasks, there is a **risk** of affecting the quality of the outputs, which could upset customers and reduce sales.

Throughput - *Task Sheet*

Class Exercise 22 - *Process step: Task Sheet.*

The operators will prepare a **task sheet** for the process step bottleneck located in Class Exercise 20.

There is a blank **Task Sheet** form in the Appendix. An Excel spreadsheet is included on the Leader Training flash drive.

Step 1 - List each task performed for the process step, in the **sequence** that they are performed.

Step 2 - Indicate which tasks are **value-adding**. Refer back to the Value-Adding section to determine what a value-adding task is.

Step 3 - Estimate the average **cycle time** for each task.

Step 4 - Add up the task cycle times to get the **total** cycle time.

Step 5 - Split the total cycle time into **value-adding** time and **non-value-adding** time.

Step 6 - Starting with the **longest** non-value-adding task, the operator should try to think of at least one way to reduce the cycle time of the task. Refer back to Sessions 13 & 14 for ideas.

Step 7 - *Estimate* the new cycle time for the tasks.

Step 8 - Add up the new task cycle times to get the new total cycle time. Split by value-adding and non-value-adding.

Session 18 - *Setup & Down Time Sheet*

To increase the throughput of a bottleneck process step:

3. Prepare a *Setup & Down Time Sheet* that lists all the setup tasks, and reasons for down time for the process step, with the following information:

   - **Description** of setup or down time.

   - The **average cycle time** for the setup or to bring the process back up from the down time event.

   - The average **frequency** of the setup task or down time event.

   - Calculate the average **minutes per day** for each setup task and down time event.

Setup & Down Time Sheet: Paint Chair Process Step							
Setup or Down Time Description	Cycle Time	Frequency	Minutes Per Day	How to Minimize	New Cycle Time	New Frequency	Minutes Per Day
Operator goes to cage to get clean rags	5 Minutes	3/Day	15	Helper brings rags 1x day	0 Minutes	0/Day	0
Clean paint gun nozzle.	5 Minutes	2/Day	10	Have clean nozzle ready	1 Minute	2/Day	2
Clean paint lines.	30 Minutes	3/Week	18	Have clean paint lines ready	5 Minutes	3/Week	3
Change paint containers	10 Minutes	2/Week	4	Have new container staged	2 Minutes	2/Week	4
Breaks	60 Minutes	1/Day	60	Stagger operator break time	0 Minutes	0/Week	0
		Total Downtime Minutes Per Day	107				9
		Seconds	6420				540

Like the task sheets, the process **operators** should prepare the **Setup & Down Time Sheet**, since they should have the greatest working **knowledge** of the process.

   - To determine the current setup **cycle times**, operators may be able to **estimate** based on their experience, or **time studies** of the tasks can be performed.

   - Precise cycle times are **not** needed. Effort should be focused on **reducing** the cycle times.

4. **Suggest ways to reduce the cycle time or frequency of the setup tasks and down time events.**

   - The methods for reducing cycle time discussed in **Sessions 13 & 14** can be used to reduce the cycle time of setups and down time events.

   - Estimate the new cycle time for each setup task or down time event.

   - Estimate the new **frequency** for each setup task or down time event.

   - Calculate the new minutes per day for each setup task and down time event.

Throughput - *Down Time Event Log*

Down time log

To help determine the down time events for the **Setup & Down Time Sheet,** a log of down time events should be created that lists each down time event and the time it takes to bring the process back up.

		Time Process	Time Process	
Date	**Down Time Event Description**	**Down**	**Up**	**Down Time**
2/20/2013	Clogged paint lines	3:27 PM	4:00 PM	0:33
2/20/2013	Clogged nozzle	10:08 AM	10:13 AM	0:05
2/20/2013	Clogged nozzle	2:33 PM	2:39 PM	0:06
2/21/2013	Turntable motor shorted	9:15 AM	11:25 AM	2:10

Down Time Event Log: Paint Chair Process Step

Down time events occur when a process has an **unscheduled** stop. Some down time events may reoccur often, like the **clogged nozzle** in the log shown above. Some down time events may be one-time events or occasional events, like equipment failure.

Since down time events are unscheduled, a **Down Time Event Log** will help to determine the amount of down time over periods of time. The log will also help determine the cycle time to resolve the events and bring the process up.

A blank Down Time Event Log is included in the Appendix. An Excel file is included on the Leader Training flash drive.

Throughput - *Setup & Down Time Sheet*

Class Exercise 23 - *Process step: Setup & Down Time Sheet.*

The operators will prepare a Setup & Down Time Sheet for the process step bottleneck located in *Class Exercise 20*.

There is a blank **Setup & Down Time Sheet** form in the Appendix. An Excel spreadsheet is included on the Leader Training flash drive.

Step 1 - List each setup task performed for the process step.

Step 2 - Estimate the average cycle time and frequency of the setup tasks.

Step 3 - Calculate the average minutes per day spent on each setup task.

Step 4 - List any recent down time events for the process step.

Step 5 - Unless down time event data is available, estimate the average cycle time and frequency for each type of event.

Step 6 - Add up the average minutes spent per day on setup and down time events.

Step 7 - Suggest ways to reduce each setup and down time event.

Step 8 - Estimate the new cycle time and frequency of each event.

Step 9 - Calculate the new minutes per day, and add them up.

Throughput - *Process Step Capacity Sheet*

Calculating Capacity - *Optional*

Using the *Task Sheet* and the *Setup and Down Time Sheet*, a capacity sheet calculates the daily throughput:

- The sheet will help determine if the suggested changes to task cycle time, setup and down time will increase throughput enough to meet sales demand.

- It will also **validate** the estimates used to complete the Task Sheets and the Setup and Down Time Sheets.

- The Excel file included with the *Leader Training* will automatically do the calculation after the *Task Sheet* data and the *Setup and Down Time Sheet* data are entered.

In the example below, daily throughput is calculated to be **410** chairs per day based on the *estimates* of task cycle time and setup and down time minutes. **Actual throughput** is **390** chairs per day, a difference of 20 chairs.

Capacity Sheet: Paint Chair Process Step		
	Current Throughput	New Throughput
Shift Minutes	480	480
Break Minutes	-50	-50
Setup & Down time/shift	-47	-9
Total Minutes Available	**383**	**421**
Seconds Available	22,980	25,260
Total Cycle Time - Seconds	**56**	**30**
Batch Size	1	1
Daily Throughput: Chairs Per Day	**410**	**842**
Actual Throughput	**390**	**805**
Difference	**-20**	**-37**

The difference indicates that either task cycle times were understated, or setup and down time minutes were underestimated, and the estimates need to be increased.

Throughput - *Removing Bottlenecks*

Increasing Throughput & Bottleneck Management

We just discussed in detail **three tools** that are used to increase the throughput of bottleneck process steps:

- Task sheet
- Setup and Down Time Sheet
- Downtime Log

It may appear at this time that a lot of data and effort is needed just to eliminate a bottleneck.

Consider:

- These tools need only to be used on the **process steps** that have **throughput** that is **less than** sales demand.
- The sheets are prepared by the **operators**, who should **already know** most of the data needed to complete the sheets.
- After preparing the sheets a few times, operators should be **able to discern** how to **increase the throughput** of a bottleneck process step **without** preparing the sheets in detail.
- Increasing sales by increasing throughput can significantly **increase profits**.
- Locating and removing bottlenecks, is usually the quickest and lowest cost way to **increase production capacity**. The alternative is to invest a lot of time, effort and money in additional equipment, inventory and floor space.

Repeat:

- As one bottleneck is **removed**, a different process step will become the **new bottleneck**.
- **Locate** the new bottleneck process step.
- **Repeat** the discussed steps until the throughput of **all process steps** are at least equal to customer **sales demand**.

Session 19 - *Variability*

Process Variability

Variability is the measure of process **consistency**.

For example:

- If the output ranges from 15 oz. of water to 16.5 oz., the **output variability is 1.5 oz.**.

- If process cycle time is sometimes as short as 8 minutes and sometimes as long as 10 minutes, the cycle time variability is 2 minutes.

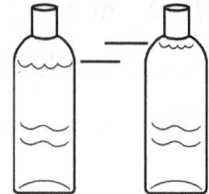

Variability causes the following types of problems:

- **Customer complaints** and returns.
- **Late** orders.
- Inconsistent cycle time or throughput.
- Outputs that have to be **scrapped** or **reworked** due to unacceptable quality.
- Operator **frustration** with equipment, raw materials, or other operators.

Reducing variability by making processes operate more consistently:

- Improves **customer satisfaction** leading to more sales.
- Reduces the need for **inventory.**
- Reduces operator **frustration** with processes.
- Reduces the **cost** to manage processes.

Variability can be broken down into three types:

- **Input variability** - The consistency of process inputs.
- **Process variability** - The consistency of processes.
- **Output variability** - The consistency of process outputs.

If the **inputs** to a process are consistent and the **process** operates in a consistent manner, the **outputs** should be consistent.

Variability

Class Exercise 24 - *Process variability.*

The operators are asked to identify ways in which the **outputs** of the process from Class Exercise 3 can **vary**.

- Use this exercise to ensure that the operators **understand** variability.

The second question asks **how** the operators determine if the **outputs are acceptable**.

- What tools and **processes** are used to determine if process outputs are of acceptable quality?

- This will be discussed further when we get to **critical measurements**.

Session 20 - *Reducing Process Variability*

Reducing Process Variability

Identify problems caused by process variability:

- *Late* customer orders.
- Customer *complaints* and returns.
- Outputs that have to be *scrapped* or reworked due to *unacceptable quality*.
- Inconsistent cycle time or throughput.
- Operator *complaints* about equipment, raw materials, processes or other workers.

Prioritize and correct the problems caused by process variability:

- Prepare a *Pareto chart* of the variability problems.
- Do *root cause* analyses of the most common problems.
- Develop *action items* to remove each root cause.

Reducing Process Variability

Class Exercise 25 - *Process variability problems.*

The operators list some of the **problems** caused by variability.

- Use this question to ensure that the operators see the **connection** between variability and problems.
- Some of the problems may already be on your **problem list**.

For **question 2**, the operators select one of the process variability problems, based on impact, and then draw a **fishbone diagram** to locate all the root causes.

To prioritize and select a problem you can use these methods:

- **Pareto** chart of the problems. Data would be needed.
- Greatest impact based on a **group** discussion.
- Consider that **upset customers** can have a big impact on sales and profits.

Work through drawing a fishbone diagram.

- It takes some effort, but much will be **learned** from the exercise.
- The needed **corrective actions** will become obvious.

Action items assigned.

- **What** needs to be done, as determined by the completed fishbone diagram?
- **Who #1** has the greatest **knowledge** needed to complete the action items?
- **What resources** will be needed, including employee time?
- **Who #2** in **management** will ensure the resources are made available?
- **When** will each action item be complete?

Session 21 - *Critical Measurements*

Critical Measurements

Some measurements are critical for determining if **outputs are satisfactory** to customers, external and **internal**. An **internal customer** is the downstream process that receives the outputs of a process. Processes should **consistently** create outputs that are satisfactory.

- **Identify** the critical attributes/measurements, based on what your **customers need** and **expect**.

- Set **standards** for critical measurements. What is the range that is **acceptable** by customers?

- Clearly document the standards using a **Critical Measurement grid**.

Critical Measurements: Bottle Fill Process Step							
Product Description	Critical Attribute	Target Measurement	Tolerance	Minimum Acceptable	Maximum Acceptable	How to Measure	How Often
8 oz bottle of water	Volume of water	8.1 oz	+/- 0.1	8.0 oz	8.2 oz	Grad Cylinder	After setup & every 3000
12 oz bottle of water	Volume of water	12.1 oz	+/- 0.1	12.0 oz	12.2 oz	Grad Cylinder	After setup & every 3000
16 oz bottle of water	Volume of water	16.1 oz	+/- 0.1	16.0 oz	16.2 oz	Grad Cylinder	After setup & every 2000
32 oz bottle of water	Volume of water	32.1 oz	+/- 0.1	32.0 oz	32.2 oz	Grad Cylinder	After setup & every 2000

- There is a blank form in the Appendix and in the Excel file included with the Leader Training flash drive.

- **Post** the standards so process operators can quickly reference them.

- Develop tools and methods so operators can **quickly measure** the outputs to determine if they are acceptable.

- **Go/no-go gauges** can be a foolproof way to quickly measure the acceptability of outputs.

Variability - *Critical Measurements*

Class Exercise 26 - *Critical Measurements.*

The operators identify some of the critical measurements for the processes they work with, and fill out a Critical Measurement grid for one of the measurements.

Identifying critical measurements:

- The measurements should be critical to **satisfying** internal customers or end customers.
- They could be related to the variability **problems** listed in Class Exercise 25.

Internal customers:

- Make sure the operators understand the concept of **internal customer**.
- An internal customer is another area of the company that **receives the outputs** of a process, either to process the outputs further, or to sell to the external customer.

Critical Measurement grid:

- The operators may need help getting all the information needed to complete the grid.
- **Invite** any employees who would have the needed information to attend the class.

Session 22 - *Critical Measurement Rejects*

Critical Measurement Rejects

When critical measurements are in effect, there will be outputs that fall outside of the acceptable range and will be rejected. To reduce process rejects, reject data needs to be collected.

- Track rejects using a ***Reject Log***.

Reject Log: Bottle Fill Process Step								
Date	Time	Product	Attribute Measured	Actual Measurement	Quantity Rejected	Cause of Rejects	Corrective Action Taken	Downtime Minutes
4/18/2013	10:03 AM	16 oz bottle of water	Volume of water	15.9 oz	50	Filler calibration	Stop line, Recalibrate filler.	3 Mins
4/18/2013	2:23 PM	32 oz bottle of water	Volume of water	32.3 oz	110	Plunger leak	Stop line, Replace plunger.	11 Mins
4/18/2013	3:01 PM	32 oz bottle of water	Volume of water	31.9 oz	27	Filler calibration	Stop line, Recalibrate filler.	5 Mins

- A blank form is in the appendix and in the Leader Training flash drive.
- After enough reject data has been collected, make a ***Pareto chart*** of the reject types.
- Do a ***root cause*** analysis of the leading type of rejects.
- Assign ***action items*** to correct the root causes.

Variability - *Critical Measurement Run Chart*

Critical Measurement Run Charts

A *Critical Measurement Run Chart* tracks the history of a measurement. It is similar to the run chart discussed in Session 5, except there is a *target value*, an *upper control limit* and a *lower control limit*.

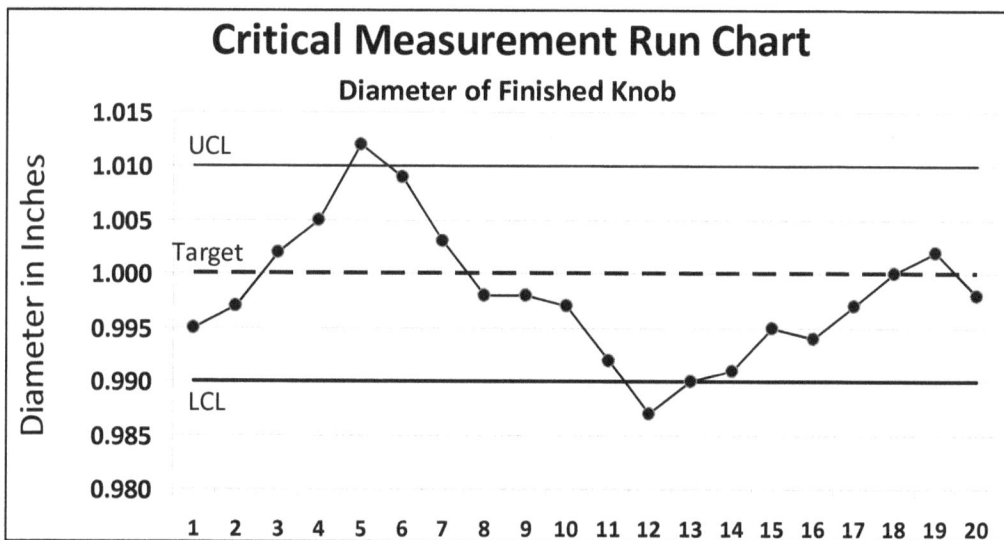

- Measurements that fall between the upper and lower control limits are *acceptable*.

- Measurements that fall outside of the upper and lower control limits are considered *unacceptable*, and corrective action needs to be taken.

- As the process improves, you should expect the measurement to move consistently *closer* to the target value.

In the critical measurement run chart above, the diameter of one-inch knobs produced by a process are sampled and measured 20 times each shift. The upper control limit is 1.01". The lower control limit is 0.99". Samples 5 and 12 fell outside of the control limits, so those knobs would be *rejected* and the process would need to be *corrected* on both occasions.

Ideally, action should be taken after measurements 4 and 11, when the measurements are *trending* towards the upper control limit or lower control limit, to avoid producing rejects.

Session 23 - *Standard Operating Procedures*

Standard Operating Procedures (SOP)

Each process should be performed consistently by following the **best available practice**, even when different operators are performing the process.

- Document the best available practice using a **Standard Operating Procedure (SOP)**.

  - **Describe** each task.

  - Detailed **instructions** of how to perform each task using the best available methods.

  - Use **diagrams** and pictures as needed to clarify the instructions.

  - Use any format that works best for the situation.

Standard Operating Procedure: Paint Chair Process Step Effective Date: 3/18/2013		
Task #	Task Description	Instructions
1	Set dolly on turntable	Set dolly on turntable with beveled edge adjacent to the raised turntable lip. Fig. 1.
2	Set chair on dolly	Set chair on dolly with all legs resting in indentations. Front legs fit in indentations closest to the beveled edge of the dolly. Fig 2.
3	Switch on turntable	
4	Pick up spray gun from table	
5	Wipe nozzle with cloth	Wipe clean the front of the spray gun nozzle with a clean rag.

Figure 1

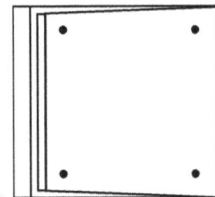

Figure 2

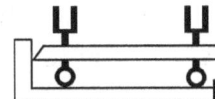

- SOPs should be **stored** in a manner that makes them quick and easy for operators to access and reference.

- The most **experienced** operators should participate in developing the procedures.

- All operators should agree to **follow** the standard operating procedures.

- **Listen** to operator suggestions for improving the procedures.

- **Update** the operating procedures as they are improved.

Variability - *Statistical Process Control*

Statistical Process Control (SPC)

There is a tool called **Statistical Process Control** that can be used for reducing variability to very small amounts.

Any operation that wants to **minimize variability** should have at least one employee who is trained in SPC.

Reducing input variability:

- **Inspect** raw materials as they are received from suppliers, using **critical measurements** as discussed in Sessions 21 & 22.
- Work with **suppliers** to ensure consistent quality and delivery cycle time.
- Track **on-time performance** failures by your suppliers using a Pareto chart.
- Collaborate with suppliers to fix the **root causes** of delivery on-time failures.

Reducing Variability Recap:

Reducing variability is critical for increasing the demand for your products, and increasing profits.

We've discussed several tools for reducing variability, it may seem overwhelming:

- Take it one step at a time.
- Start by identifying and removing process variability **problems**.
- The problems will identify where you need to document **critical measurements**.
- After a critical measurement is in place, start a **reject log** for the measurement.
- Writing **standard operating procedures** takes considerable time, so start with the process steps where needed most. Later, after processes have been **streamlined** and there are more resources available, begin a widespread SOP program.
- If you need to reduce variability to minuscule amounts, employ **control charts** and **SPC**.
- Operator **participation** can make reducing variability a rewarding experience, instead of an unpleasant struggle.

Session 24 - *Inventory*

Inventory

Inventory types

Inventory can be broken down into four types:

- **In-process inventory** - Materials within a process:

    - Being *modified* during a process step,
  or
    - *Waiting* in a *queue* for the next process step.

- **Raw materials** - Unprocessed materials *waiting to be input* into a process.

- **Finished goods inventory** - The final outputs of a process, *waiting to be sold* and delivered to a customer.

The benefits of reducing inventory:

- Inventory ties up cash. Reducing inventory increases *cash flow*.
- For companies facing cash flow shortages, reducing inventory can be *critical*.
- It takes *time and effort* to track and manage inventory, increasing costs.
- Inventory can be *damaged*, go bad or become obsolete, increasing costs.
- Inventory takes up *space*.
- Freeing up space by reducing inventory will make it easier to *streamline* the physical layout of your processes.

In-Process Inventory

In-process Inventory

Many of the same actions that **reduce cycle time** will also reduce in-process inventory. The section on in-process inventory is partly redundant, but it **reinforces** the benefits of reducing cycle time.

Some reasons why we have in-process inventory:

- Processes take time. Inventory needs to be within process steps during processing time so it can be modified and have **value added**.

- Processes usually require a number of tasks to be completed in a particular sequence. In-process inventory allows multiple tasks to be performed at the same time to **increase throughput**.

- Queue inventory is needed as a **buffer** when the process steps have different cycle times, and it is desired to keep all operators busy at all times.

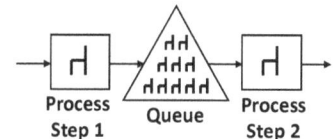

- Queue inventory is created when processes are done in **batches**. The larger the batch size, the greater queue inventory will be.

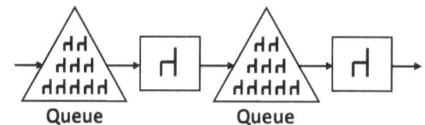

- Queue inventory may accumulate before **bottleneck** process steps.

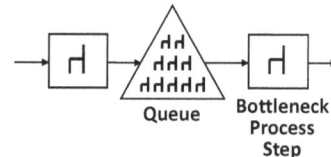

In-Process Inventory

Class Exercise 27 - *In-process inventory.*

For *Class Exercise 14* the operators counted the units of inventory within a process in order to calculate the cycle time of the process. For this exercise, the operators will split the inventory by *queue* inventory and *process step* inventory.

- This will highlight for the operators how much inventory is having **value added** and how much inventory is sitting idle, **consuming space** and **cash** flow.

- For many operations, most of the inventory is **queue inventory**, which means there is a lot of **opportunity** to reduce in-process inventory, reduce queue time, free up space and generate cash flow.

- If there happens to be a **small amount** of queue inventory within a process, then reducing the inventory for that process probably does not need to be a priority.

Session 25 - Reducing In-Process Inventory

The process formula rearranged

Rearranging the **process formula** we discussed in **Session 11**, can help us to find ways to reduce inventory:

$$\text{In-Process Inventory} = \text{Cycle Time} \times \text{Throughput}$$

$$40 \text{ chairs} = 4 \text{ hours} \times 10 \text{ chairs per hour}$$

The formula shows us that:

- Reducing the **queue time** of a process will reduce queue inventory.

- Reducing **processing time** by combining process steps will reduce in-process inventory.

Reducing in-process inventory:

Queue inventory can be reduced using the same methods for reducing **queue time** already discussed in **Session 14:**

- Reducing the **transfer batch size** between process steps by using equipment such as conveyors.

- Reducing **setup time** may allow transfer batch size to be reduced.

- **Balancing** a process so that all process steps have the **same cycle time**.

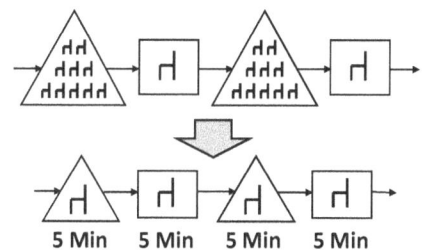

- Identifying and eliminating **bottlenecks** within the process will reduce queue inventory.

- **Issuing** inventory to a process at the same rate as the throughput of the **bottleneck** process step, will reduce queue inventory.

- **Combining process steps** so they can be performed **concurrently** instead of sequentially.

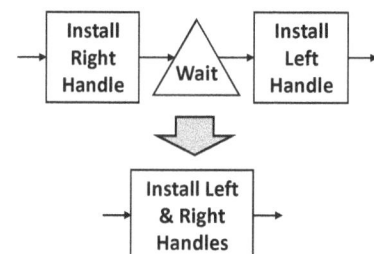

Reducing In-Process Inventory

Class Exercise 28 - *Reducing In-process inventory.*

The operators should now understand that many of the **same activities** that reduced cycle time will also reduce inventory. This exercise has the operators reflect on the suggestions they gave in **Class Exercise 18** to reduce cycle time, to determine if some of those suggestions will also reduce inventory.

- This will **reinforce** the value of reducing cycle time.

- It will show them that they **already know** how to reduce in-process inventory.

- For **part 2** of the exercise, the operators will identify which processes have a lot of queue inventory. This will locate **low hanging fruit** for reducing queue inventory and cycle time.

- **Part 3** of the exercise asks the operators for **ideas** to reduce in-process inventory. This will generate more ideas for reducing inventory and cycle time.

Session 26 - *Raw Materials Inventory*

Raw Materials Inventory.

Raw materials inventory is a **buffer** between the supplier of the materials and the processes, to ensure raw materials are available to input into the processes when needed.

Some reasons why we have raw materials inventory:

- It may be impossible to exactly **predict** when raw materials will be needed to be input into a process, so inventory needs to be waiting and **available** when needed.

- Raw materials typically come from suppliers. It may be **logistically impractical** for a supplier to deliver raw materials at the exact moment the materials are needed to be input into a process.

- Shipping materials from a supplier may have a high cost. Shipping materials in batches usually reduces the per unit **cost of shipping**.

Reducing raw materials inventory:

- Improved **controls** of raw materials inventory will allow the inventory to be reduced.

  - A **Kanban** (visual reorder point) system helps to ensure materials are ordered from suppliers in a timely manner.

- Reduce **order quantities** from suppliers.

- Work with suppliers to reduce the **cycle time** of orders.

- Work with suppliers to improve the **consistency** of supplier cycle time.

Class Exercise 29 - *Reducing raw materials inventory.*

The operators are asked to identify the **largest** raw material item, in terms of **dollars,** on hand in inventory. **Invite** the person who would have this information to attend the meeting.

- **Question 2** asks for **practical** ways of reducing the amount of inventory for the item.

- Only reduce the inventory of a raw material item when **controls** are in place to ensure that the item will always be available to input into the processes when needed.

Session 27 - Finished Goods Inventory

Finished Goods Inventory

Finished goods inventory is a *buffer* between our processes and our customer's needs, to help ensure product is *available* for our customers when they need it.

Some reasons why we have finished goods inventory:

- It may be impossible to predict exactly when customers will want our products, so finished goods inventory may be stocked, to make our products immediately available *when our customers need them.*

- Shipping product to a customer may have a high cost. Manufacturing and shipping product in batches usually reduces the per unit *cost of shipping*.

Reducing finished goods inventory:

- Reduced process *batch size* should reduce the need for finished goods inventory.

   - If once a *month* you build an amount equal to one-month's sales, your average finished goods inventory for the product will be equal to 1/2 month of sales.

   - If you build the same product *weekly*, and build an amount equal to one week's sales, your average finished goods inventory for the product will be equal to 1/2 week of sales.

- Reducing *setup time* will often allow batch sizes to be reduced.

- Better *communication* with *customers* will help improve forecasting of customer demand, allowing finished goods inventory to be reduced.

- More *consistent* process cycle time will allow finished goods inventory to be reduced.

Class Exercise 30 - *Reducing finished goods inventory.*

The operators are asked to identify the *largest* finished good item, in terms of *dollars,* on hand in inventory. *Invite* the person who would have this information to attend the meeting.

- *Question 2* asks for *practical* ways of reducing the amount of inventory for the item.

- For *question 3,* the operators consider the impact of reducing *setup time* on reducing batch size, and reducing finished goods inventory.

Session 28 - Costs

Process Costs

Reducing process costs increases **profits** and **cash flow** while reducing the impact of operations on the natural environment.

Process costs can be broken down into two types:

- **Variable Costs -** Costs that vary with output volume:
  - Process labor costs.
  - Raw material inputs.
  - Process supplies.
  - Outside services.
  - Product warranty.

- **Overhead costs -** The cost to provide process capacity. Costs that do not change, in the short term, as output changes.
  - Rent.
  - Insurance.
  - Depreciation.
  - Maintenance.
  - Outside services.

- Some costs will be partly **variable and** partly **fixed**.
  - Electricity.
  - Supplies.

Many of the activities for improving processes that have already been discussed will reduce costs:

- Reducing **injuries** will reduce labor and overhead costs.
- Reducing processing time, setup time, down time will reduce labor costs.
- Removing **bottlenecks** may reduce labor costs.
- Reducing **inventory** will reduce labor costs and overhead costs.
- Reducing **scrap**, rework, rejects and customer returns will reduce material and labor costs.

Cost Reporting

Cost Reporting

Most companies already report costs at a high level in the monthly *profit and loss statements*. *Detailed* cost reporting by department or work cell may or may not be available. It will depend on how the accounting systems are set up.

Invite a company *accountant* to present and explain the existing cost reports. Ask the operators to identify the costs that they impact.

At a minimum, cost reporting should be *split* by variable and overhead costs. Some costs, for example electricity, will have both a variable component and fixed component. If possible these costs should be split and each component reported separately.

As you progress through the workbook and improve the processes, you should expect to see both the variable per unit costs and overhead costs go down.

Fine Furniture Company
Variable Costs - January

	Cost	Cost/ Unit
Units Produced	27,106	
Labor	$43,070	$1.59
Materials	$32,026	$1.18
Hardware	$4,599	$0.17
Electricity	$4,205	$0.16
Solvents	$3,845	$0.14
Packaging	$3,706	$0.14
Freight	$3,624	$0.13
Hand Tools	$3,281	$0.12
Abrasives	$2,468	$0.09
Gloves	$1,407	$0.05
Brushes	$1,207	$0.04
Total Variable Costs	**$103,438**	**$3.82**

Reducing variable costs:

- As mentioned, improving the other process measurements will reduce labor, material and other variable costs.

Session 29 - *Reducing Costs*

- Collaborating with existing supplies or changing suppliers may be a way to reduce material or outside service costs.

Reducing overhead costs:

- *Management* usually has control over most overhead costs.
- *Improved processes* should reduce some overhead costs.
  - Reducing *inventory* will reduce the cost of managing the inventory.
  - Fewer *problems* with the processes will reduce the cost to manage the processes.
- Reduce *waste* of supplies like ear plugs, safety glasses, paper towels, and rags.
- Ask a company accountant to prepare a *twelve month* running history of overhead costs like shown below, and present to the operators.
- Ask the operators to *identify* the costs that they impact.

Fine Furniture Company
Overhead Costs

	Jan	Feb	Mar	Apr	May	Jun	Jul	Aug	Sep	Oct	Nov	Dec
Rent	18,532	18,532	18,532	18,532	18,532	18,532	18,532	18,532	18,532	18,532	20,287	20,287
Depreciation	6,235	6,235	6,235	6,235	6,235	6,308	6,308	6,964	6,964	7,185	7,185	7,258
Insurance	20,599	29,691	20,599	20,599	20,599	20,599	20,599	20,599	20,599	26,473	26,473	26,473
PPE Supplies	2,702	2,438	2,385	2,196	2,253	2,517	2,464	2,275	2,332	2,279	2,090	2,147
Outside Services	175	270	937	1,611	918	1,667	-	169	277	324	-	1,227
Repairs & Maint.	2,637	762	351	1,277	561	440	2,455	165	508	1,181	3,873	356
Supplies	3,706	3,894	1,158	4,789	3,185	2,924	2,734	2,740	3,799	1,023	4,508	2,867
Utilities-Gas	1,006	984	1,043	863	694	534	463	408	576	765	894	972
Utilities-Electricity	6,335	6,248	6,354	6,446	6,844	7,088	7,459	7,807	8,784	7,201	6,104	5,901
Utilities-Water	174	190	201	171	176	215	226	231	217	173	169	160
Telephone	675	675	550	550	550	575	575	575	575	700	700	700
Total Overhead	62,776	69,919	58,345	63,269	60,547	61,399	61,815	60,465	63,163	65,836	72,283	68,348

Reducing Costs

Class Exercise 31 - *Reducing costs.*

Ask the operators for *suggestions* to reduce costs.

- Each operator has a different *perspective*, so each one may spot *opportunities* that no one else will notice.

- *Prioritize* the opportunities and create *action items* to implement.

Recap

What we have learned:

- The **operations** level of an organization is where the organization makes its money.

- Operations consists of **processes**. Improving the processes will increase the organization's sales, profits and cash flow.

- Operator **participation** provides critical information for improving processes and will **motivate** the operators to improve the processes they work with.

- **Problems** are golden **opportunities** for improvement. The more problems you can identify the greater the opportunity.

- **Pareto charts** help to **prioritize** what problems to eliminate first.

- Use **root cause analysis** to truly correct and eliminate problems.

- The **seven process performance metrics** give clear **direction** for process improvement.

- **Run charts** clearly **communicate** if a process is improving.

- The **process formula** is useful for reducing cycle time and increasing throughput.

- Reducing **queue time** is usually the quickest way to reduce cycle time and reduce in-process inventory.

- Managing **bottleneck** process steps can reduce cycle time, increase throughput and sales, reduce inventory, increase on-time performance and reduce costs.

- Reducing **variability** will increase customer satisfaction, reduce inventory and costs.

- There are **dozens of ways** to improve processes. Which approach should be used, depends on the situation.

Getting Started

Creating a high-performance culture of continuous improvement:

Listen! - The power behind this program comes from the process operators. Your responsibility as *the leader* is to lead the program, not do all the talking. The operators can only provide the *critical information* needed if you listen to them. The more you listen, the more information they will provide, and the more they will be *motivated* to participate and assist in implementing the program.

- To maximize operator *motivation* to participate in the program and push for implementation, management should offer a *gain sharing* program to the operators, where the operators are given a percentage of the improvement to profits.

- Prepare for each meeting by *reviewing the pages* to be discussed, to ensure you understand the material.

- As mentioned earlier, the quickest and easiest way to get started is to create a *list of problems* that the process operators reveal. Use those problems to practice using Pareto charts and root cause analyses to begin eliminating the problems. This will get the operators *emotionally involved* and vested in the program, and also start improving the processes.

- *Cleaning* and immaculately *organizing* work areas will improve all seven metrics, plus it will make the other improvements easier, so cleaning and organizing work areas is usually the best way to start improving the work areas.

  Some operators will *welcome* better organization, others will *resist*, so start with those areas where the operators are supportive of improving the organizing. This should help to demonstrate to the other operators the value of clean, organized work areas.

Getting Started

- Seek *low hanging fruit*. The program discusses many different ways for improving processes. Start by using the tools that will give you rapid improvement based on *your* current situation and *needs*.

- After streamlining individual work stations then consider *reorganizing work cells* to minimize operator and material movements, and also to reduce in-process inventory.

- As the leader, you do not need to know much about the processes to get started. The operators will provide most of the information needed. *You will learn* what you need to know as you progress through the program.

- *Invite* other employees to attend sessions *if* they can provide *information* that is clearly *relevant* to what is being discussed during the session. For example:
  - Maintenance people when discussing equipment problems.
  - Sales people or customers when discussing customer complaints.
  - HR people when discussing injuries.
  - Accounting people when discussing costs.

- The important thing is to **GET STARTED**, so the organization can begin benefitting from process improvement, and *push on* at whatever pace works best for your organization's situation, until *continuous process improvement* becomes ingrained into the operating culture.

Appendix - *Pedometer Log*

Pedometer Log		
Date	**Name**	**Miles Walked**
Total Miles Walked		

Appendix - *Task Sheet*

Task Sheet:

Task #	Task Description	Cycle Time	How to Minimize	New Cycle Time
	Total Cycle Time			
	Value-Add			
	Non-Value-Add			

Appendix - *Setup & Down Time Sheet*

Setup & Down Time Sheet:

Setup or Down Time Description	Cycle Time	Frequency	Minutes Per Day	How to Minimize	New Cycle Time	New Frequency	New Minutes Per Day
Total Downtime Minutes Per Day							
Seconds							

Appendix - *Down Time Event Log*

Down Time Event Log:

Date	Down Time Event Description	Time Process Down	Time Process Up	Down Time

Appendix - *Critical Measurements Grid*

Critical Measurements:

Product Description	Critical Attribute	Target Measurement	Tolerance	Minimum Acceptable	Maximum Acceptable	How to Measure	How Often

Appendix - *Reject Log*

Reject Log:

Date	Time	Product	Attribute Measured	Acceptable Range	Actual Measurement	Quantity Rejected	Cause of Rejects	Corrective Action Taken	Downtime Minutes

Index

Index

S

Spaghetti diagram 16
Supplies for training 12

T

Throughput 36
  Bottleneck management 38
  Process formula 40

V

Value-adding 29
Variability 50
  Critical measurements 54
  Reject log 56
  Standard operating procedure 58
  Statistical process control 59

www.ingramcontent.com/pod-product-compliance
Lightning Source LLC
Chambersburg PA
CBHW082059210326
41521CB00032B/2541